Science
and
Religion

Science
and
Religion

By Ferdinand Brunetière

Translated by Erik Butler.

ODD VOLUMES

of

The Fortnightly Review

LES BROUZILS

2016

in cooperation with

THE CHAVAGNES STUDIUM PRESS

Chavagnes-en-Paillers.

Odd Volumes of *The Fortnightly Review*

Editorial:

Château du Ligny

2 rue Georges Clémenceau

85260 Les Brouzils

France

info@fortnightlyreview.co.uk

ODD VOLUMES
www.fortnightlyreview.co.uk

in cooperation with

THE CHAVAGNES STUDIUM PRESS

www.chavagnes.org

ISBN 978-0692519011

TABLE OF CONTENTS

INTRODUCTION

SCIENCE AND FICTION

Connaissez-vous Brunetière? — "Do you know Brunetière?" — asked literary historian Antoine Compagnon some twenty years ago.[i] Needless to say, the question was rhetorical. Ferdinand Brunetière (1849-1906), who contributed to the influential *Revue des Deux Mondes* starting in the mid-1870s and later assumed the journal's directorship, became an "immortal" in 1893. This title, which decorates members of the Académie Française, has an anachronistic ring. Consecration also suggests detachment from the world. As such, it is perfectly suited to Brunetière. His writings exemplify the cultural and intellectual conflicts that defined the *fin-de-siècle* although — and because — they stood at odds with general opinion. Even if they have largely fallen into oblivion, their provocative potential remains as strong as ever. The Third Republic incubated twentieth-century Europe: accelerating industrialization, democracy, mass movements, colonialist projects, nationalism, anti-Semitism, secularism, and more still. Now, at the outset of a new millennium, perhaps Brunetière's day has come again. At any rate, the world's problems have persisted: their "immortality" leaves no room for doubt whatsoever.

Brunetière made a name for himself as a critic with classical sensibilities, especially by taking issue with the fashionably scandalous naturalism of the times. This school, Brunetière argued, lost itself in tedious — and uninspiring — attention to matters too coarse to yield anything of refinement, beauty, or insight. Overexcited nervous tissue admits thorough and methodical investigation, but if novels and plays amount to case studies of morbid and pathological states, then the "doctors" who write them have done nothing of value. Brunetière was doctrinaire, but he was doctrinaire along idiosyncratic lines. Although he opposed Émile Zola's efforts to turn science into art, he also tried his hand at a theory of the evolution of literary genres inspired by Darwinian theory. In the notorious Dreyfus Affair, he held that the accused was guilty; at the same time, he shunned the conspiratorial and bigoted vociferations popular among the luckless officer's opponents. Almost entirely self-taught, Brunetière commanded respect and inspired revulsion in equal measure in the republic of letters; in keeping with the vagaries of the political climate during the tempestuous *Belle Époque*, he basked in glory and was showered with opprobrium.[ii]

Science and Religion, which appeared five years before Brunetière converted to Catholicism in 1900, surprised many of his contemporaries. His admiration for the eloquent seventeenth-century theologian Bossuet notwithstanding, Brunetière had counted as a rationalist until this point. If prone to asceticism and pedantry, he ultimately enjoyed the reputation of a freethinker. Indeed, the arguments advanced in the essay at hand — which was written after a visit to the pope in 1894 — do not conform to dogma, even though they advocate the Church's authority: Brunetière, it seems, arrived at his conclusions by thinking matters through as soberly as possible. There is not the slightest hint of spirituality in the pages to follow. While conducting a vigorous polemic against faith in secular improvement, *Science and Religion* strikes a balance between age-old moral commandments and the practical demands of modernity. For Brunetière, "science" and "religion" need not count as opposites. To employ a philosophical idiom that is not the author's own, they admit dialectical resolution.

I. THEN...

By any human measure, science is as old as the stars. One of the earliest learned pursuits, if not the first, was the study of heavenly bodies. The ancient practice has only gained in popularity in the modern world: after millennia of astrology, the Soviet Union launched an unsuspecting dog into orbit, and, about a decade later, the United States put a man on the moon. But even if humans colonized another planet, one thing would not change: no one would really know "what it all means." Many would rave about the significance of the accomplishment, but their kind already does so about occurrences on earth. Space may be the final frontier, but it is also the first: a boundless expanse that resists the schemes of human intelligence.

Brunetière lived and died before the "space race" invested the heavens with the hopes and dreams of nations and ideologies bent on conquering the world below by way of the firmament above. Every word that he wrote still holds today: mortal minds can only conceive (in fact, the term is a misnomer) the infinite negatively. The receding horizon of the macrocosm mirrors the vanishing point of the microcosm. As human existence moves in a foreign, material element on the earth, so it must where there is no air to breathe at all. By definition, we, as mortal beings, inhabit what Saint Augustine called the "region of unlikeness." Eternal identities — Platonic forms — can appear only to God.

Brunetière's quarrel is with "contemporary positivism," which fails to recognize what a later idiom would call the structural limitations of human knowledge. "Fact" does not mean "truth," for one. What is more, the sciences, which mark out fields of endeavor with fewer points of contact than the uninitiated might think, "are incapable — I wouldn't say of resolving, so much as posing, in fitting manner, the sole questions of import: those concerning the origin of man, the law of his conduct, and his future destiny. The unknowable surrounds us, envelops us, and holds us in its grasp." The element of human life is obscurity; any light we project comes from one point and extends to another. Even a thousand rays are just line segments on a plane; a further dimension is missing. The fires of human ingenuity may describe figures, like the constellations in the sky, and these figures may suggest meaning, but even a "solar myth" is just that — a myth. First and final causes lie beyond our ken.

The "destiny" to which Brunetière appeals would mean a big picture comprised of isolated perspectives: those of individuals, learned societies, and, indeed,

Society writ large. The author commends Leo XIII for seeking such a synthesis. The *savants* he takes to task do not have a sufficiently broad outlook, for they purchase knowledge by narrowing their focus: anatomists examine anatomy, chemists study chemistry, physicists study physics, etc. What Brunetière says in a related context applies here: such undertakings amount to so many "tautologies" — they map out terrain and fill in blanks, yet their content has already been determined formally: the questions asked already presuppose answers of a certain nature. Reliant upon theories and models, the sciences exclude whatever proves incalculable — "mystery" and "grace" in a theological dimension, and "morality" in the realm of human action.

The criticism Brunetière aims at those who bring "the analogies offered by natural history" to elucidate the life of communities extends to those who would apply such analogies to politics. Socialists, for example, advocate the "extension of state power" to regulate labor, commerce, and justice. This, too, represents a mode of abstraction — engineering that may offer benefits, to be sure, but does not include even a placeholder for spontaneity or surprise. The "science" of guaranteeing social equality yields a castle in the sky, at best, and "tyrannical" intervention in people's lives, at worst. "[T]he 'social contract' is not an insurance contract" — and even if it were, the claims of human beings, ever at odds with each other, could not be processed in advance.

Reason — the vaunted faculty of the eighteenth century, which in turn became the instrument steering the advances of the nineteenth — breaks down wholes into parts. Brunetière acknowledges its analytical merits, but he warns against inferences that fashion new totalities out of the elements coming from disassembled material.

> [I]f it's true that science has sought to replace "religion" for the last hundred years, then science has lost the match — both for the time being and for the foreseeable future. Unable to provide even an initial response to the sole questions of interest, neither science in general nor the individual disciplines — physics, the study of nature, philology, or history — is entitled to what they have claimed for a century: to govern life in the present.

"Individual disciplines" are just that: individual. The unity they project, singly or in combination, is hypothetical. The sciences offer promissory notes, as it were, yet these highly specialized and technical documents do not have inherent, immediate, or universal value; only experts can appreciate their worth, but these same experts are often the first to contest the importance of their peers' and forebears' findings. The gold standard — Truth — does not circulate.

The same holds in matters of religion. "Protestantism surely has 'reason' on its side," but it occupies a comparatively insecure position, for "religion is not philosophy. " As the very name suggests, Protestantism is adversarial and, at the same time, obsessed with its own justification. Forgoing the reassurances of the Church as it has evolved over millennia, "[t]he sinner grows confused, suffers injury, and, to speak with Luther's words, is engulfed by conscience of his unworthiness, terror before his Judge, and fear of damnation." In contrast, "'logic' speaks for Catholicism": here, reflective discourse (*logos*) weighs and evaluates propositions in terms of an overarching set of rules that transcends the hustle and bustle of intellectual commerce and "preoccupation with faith that destroys hope." Catholicism has deep roots, and its branches stretch high above individual men and women. If it seems to spread darkness at times, one should recall that shade can also provide rest that quickens body and mind.

Instead of "losing heretics forever," Catholicism, with its scholastic debates — and even its inquisitions

— seeks to sift the proverbial wheat from the chaff and incorporate only practices and views that have withstood sustained scrutiny. The progressive cleansing of souls in the afterlife has a correlate in the purification of thought on earth. Likewise, the syncretic aspects of the Church — which opponents fault for its legions of saints and innumerable relics — attests to an attitude of "reconciliation" that would find a place for all and sundry in the "many... mansions" of the Lord's house. The rock this house is built on is revelation, the age-old foundation of the Bible. "Whatever it may be, something in the history of the 'people of God' is not found in the history of any other people." Accordingly, this history — in which Jews and Gentiles alike acknowledge a higher order and calling — must stand at both the beginning and at the end of all reflection on individual and communal life. Brunetière suggests that those who hope for a technical, man-made solution to the world's problems are idolators before a golden calf.

II....AND NOW

Inasmuch as Brunetière appeals to timeless principles instead of mutable facts, what he wrote over a hundred years ago "applies" (in the jargon of our times) even now. Some of the "failures" he enumerates count as self-evident — to the extent that they receive any attention at all. Philology, for example, epitomizes academic vainglory, and therefore obsolescence. The "hard sciences" continue to receive honors, yet largely to the extent that their discoveries lend themselves to practical use. Observation of the Higgs boson has failed to move worlds. And when an evolutionary biologist like Richard Dawkins claims to debunk the "God delusion," his non-argument hardly warrants discussion. However illusory "God" may be, the Deity is a social, anthropological, and historical given; dogmatic denial is bad science, if not mortal sin.

Indeed, the signs of scientific bankruptcy are clearer than ever. Ironically, the evidence remains hidden because the portents are only growing in number and frequency. In contrast to the nineteenth century, when positivism promised further findings that would yield a coherent totality one day, overflowing data is now crowding out the little that remains of the "spirit" of our age. The universe, we are told, is expanding; this is the otherworldly correlate of mounting inflation and "obesity," as Jean Baudrillard would say.[iii] "Black holes" or "dark matter" somewhere beyond the planet's atmosphere hardly suggest relief from all the gas, whether it's methane or cloud technology, that clogs the air below. Meanwhile — and with an intensity that all but destroys one's ability to pause and appreciate the scale of the phenomenon — a host of hypermediated, automatic connections has descended upon the globe. Swollenness and bloating, both literal and figural, are omnipresent.

Positivism may be dated, but positivity is not.[iv] The matter is hardly as gladsome as it may sound: the signals, impulses, and images that bombard a guileless yet complicit humanity have a deracinating effect far more profound than the innovations that, in Max Weber's phrase, "disenchanted" the world when modernity was young. Computerized, automated technology works factitious magic to prevent the relevant questions from even being posed; it is hard to concentrate for long enough to think. Advertising pops up everywhere in the perpetually distended internet, offering countless products and services claiming to fix any problem at all — whether physical, psychic, or economic. One can check police records, credit history, family genealogy, or current events just like that, yet none of this information provides an anchor for being. Social media enable one to make more "friends" in the course of an afternoon than people used to have over a whole lifetime. Helpful suggestions based on browsing history lure online shoppers deeper and deeper down a wormhole of mutually re-inforcing narcissism and consumerism. Notoriously, chat rooms and digital forums act as echo chambers for buttressing views already held. Facebook offers no alternative to "liking" a post besides scrolling on to the next one to see if it suits the fancy of the mod-ern-day *scriba indoctus* better.[v]

Thanks to the feedback loop of a wired existence, human beings feed data to machines that are becom-ing smarter and smarter…. Whether people are be-coming dumber or not, they are certainly in thrall of something that would have qualified as wholly alien — practically extraterrestrial — mere decades ago. In the age of "Google," carbon-based organisms spend a good part of waking life amidst disembodied, viral doubles. Thanks to television and Hollywood, the host proliferates every day, like a biblical plague. "Virtual reality" proves harder and harder to escape — as does its "really real" effects. Even people in the so-called developing world, without all the lures and blandish-ments of Silicon Valley, are prey to globalized market forces coordinated by these same imposturous instru-ments; their invasive power far exceeds the potential of yesteryear's colonialist administrations, which still relied on paperwork and postage stamps to function.

A vanishingly small number of elites may enjoy — and even take Calvinist pride in — the rewards offered by such a flexible system of enterprise. Many more, incapable of picturing anything else, may disport themselves in a fool's paradise of pornography and punditry. Yet a teeming mass of humanity comes away empty-handed from towering modern-day pyramids and graven images. It is regrettable, but not wholly inexplicable, when entrepreneurs of another stripe — terrorists — conjure up the power of the Deity in the form that first made mankind aware of something immeasurably greater than itself: destruction so senseless it can only come from the Author of the World, with the power to make and unmake life. The denial of any and all kinds of salutary negativity in doses — rest, idleness, and unproductivity — engenders nihilism.

When Brunetière wrote that "battle looms," he was not exaggerating. Two World Wars, if nothing else, should have proven as much; the struggles for national liberation that emerged when European empires collapsed have dotted the globe with expanding theaters of conflict. The economic and cultural imperialism of gung-ho American capitalism has begotten a market that can operate perfectly well without its creator. Fundamentalism has only flourished in response to "progress" (including, not too long ago, the "scientific socialism" espoused by the Soviet Union). Such starry-eyed atavism — along with doomed efforts to combat it — guarantees more and more altars of human sacrifice. Meanwhile, "interactive" software induces passivity far more deadening than the "opiate of the masses" derided by eighteenth- and nineteenth-century secularists.

The fictions of contemporary science are at least as dull as any of the novels Brunetière faulted for lack of vision. Logic speaks for the Church, if only because the alternative is schizophrenia: catatonic stupor or hyperactivity. With so many demiurges generating pixelated fireworks for entertainment and — supposedly — instruction, the wise would do well to look beyond their computer screens. Almost all the lights one sees in the sky may have burned out long ago, but their soft glow, even if it means nothing at all, has already lasted an eternity in comparison to the glare engulfing our planet. Religion is like gravity: without it, everything flies off — and often sooner than later — into the void.

Erik Butler

SCIENCE AND RELIGION

Last January, when I published the article hereby presented as an independent volume, I was hoping it would be read, but — modesty obliges — I wasn't expecting to provoke so much commotion.

The truth is, the question concerned, if not the "bankruptcy" of Science, then the "failures" it has experienced with respect to at least some of the promises it has made. That said, I was not the first to employ the term; some ten others had already pronounced it publicly. I lauded, to the best of my ability, the generous initiative — or apostolic audacity — of Pope Leo XIII. Far from being one of the first, I was, on the contrary, one of the last to do so, and, in this regard, I have only one regret: to have waited too long. After all, quite summarily and quite discretely, I am suggesting that Christianity, in spite of our scholars and exegetes, is still a force to be reckoned with; I thought

I was doing nothing but remarking something self-evident. None of that was terribly new or particularly extraordinary.

But because the article gave rise to such a tumult — and since, after three months, neither the lull of the New Year, a minister's fall, the resignation of the President of the Republic, the election of M. Brisson, Carnival, Lent, nor the trial of M. Coquelin and the *Comédie française* drew journalists' attention to other matters — I was finally convinced that I had said things more interesting than I believed. Therefore, I am reprinting it.

I have made no corrections — even of style — and have contented myself to add sizeable notes that more or less double the length. May they also double its import!

4 April 1895

———————————————

On November 27 of the year that just ended, I had the honor of being granted a private audience with His Holiness Pope Leo XIII. Surely no one will expect me to commit the indiscretion or impropriety, here or anywhere else, of divulging what he deigned share.[1] Since the visit has naturally prompted a few reflections on my part, I consider it opportune — or *timely,* as one says — to consign them to writing. That is all the following pages offer, and I hope the reader will not seek anything else.

I

Not long ago, learned incredulity passed for a sign, if not proof, of superior intelligence and intellectual vigor. The importance of "religions," and certainly of "religious sentiment," was acknowledged in the development of mankind. Indeed, it was a point of pride to have moved beyond eighteenth-century wit. While professing personal disbelief, the learned never tired of faulting Voltaire, Diderot, and Condorcet for the injuriousness of their anti-Christian polemics, the dishonesty of their arguments, and the narrowness of their philosophy.[2] All the same — following Auguste Comte and his whole school — the "theological stage" counted as what I would call the embryonic phase of the mind's life. Maybe a few physiologists or anthropologists remain convinced of the same, still today. "Religions," a recent book affirms, "are purified relics of superstition…. The value of a civilization is inversely proportional to religious fervor…. All intellectual progress corresponds to a reduction of the supernatural in the world…. The future belongs to science." These lines date from 1892, but the spirit that dictated them is some twenty or thirty years older.[3]

What has happened since then? What mute labor has occurred in the depths of modern thought? In due course, we will discuss the "bankruptcy of science." Scholars grow indignant at these words, and the laboratories echo in laughter. "After all," they say, "what promises have physics or chemistry not kept — or surpassed? Our sciences were born only yesterday, and in less than a century they have changed the features of life. Give them time to mature! What's more, who is it that presumes to speak of bankruptcy or failure? What do they know of science? What advance in mechanics or natural history does their name decorate? Did they invent the telephone or discover the vaccine for croup? That's what we'd like to know before answering. Finally, if a member of our learned society who's a bit fantastical or adventurous in spirit has undertaken unapproved activities in the name of science, is science itself to be accused? Common sense, which Descartes deemed 'the most evenly distributed thing in the world,' is, in fact, as rare as may be imagined — rarer than talent, and perhaps as uncommon as genius. We'll gladly concede that some great men have lacked it." Such is the reasoning of those who wish to see "the bankruptcy of science" as nothing more than a striking metaphor. Nor can I say they are entirely mistaken.[4]

Yet they are not entirely right, either. Whatever distinction they have tried to make between the common sense of "true" scientists and the vexing temerity of others, the fact remains that science has promised to renew the "face of the earth" more than once. "I believe I have proven that it is possible," Condorcet wrote just a hundred years ago, "to grant intellectual discernment a nearly universal quality, … such that the habitual condition of man, in a people as a whole, is to be led by truth, … subject in conduct to the laws of morality, … and nourished by gentle and pure sentiments." Moreover, he added, "This is the point to which works of genius *and the progress of enlightenment* must *unfailingly* lead."[5] It might be objected that Condorcet was a mere encyclopedist. Yet that's exactly what I mean! Renan, at least when starting his career, affirmed the very same: "Science will always remain the gratification of the noblest striving in our nature, curiosity; *it will always supply man with the sole means of improving his lot.*" At another point in the same book — *The Future of Science*, whose very title announces a whole program — he declares: "the *scientific organization of humanity*" — the emphasis is his own — "offers the final word of modern science, its bold but legitimate pretension."[6] These statements, I should think, make quite a promise! They reach a bit further than the ambitions of a chemist or a physicist — and they are the reason why it has been claimed that science is bankrupt.[7]

But let us look at the matter more closely. The physical, or natural, sciences promised to dispel "mystery." As it turns out, they have not only failed to do so, it is clear today that they will never shine a light on mystery at all. They are incapable — I wouldn't say of resolving, so much as posing, in fitting manner, the sole questions of import: those concerning the origin of man, the law of his conduct, and his future destiny. The unknowable surrounds us, envelops us, and holds us in its grasp; from the laws of physics and the results of physiology we can derive nothing to understand any part of it. As much as anyone, I admire Darwin's immortal works; when the influence of his doctrine is likened to Newton's discoveries, I gladly agree. But still! To say we are perhaps descended from apes, or that apes and human beings may have a common ancestor — has this moved us forward or answered the real question of our origins? "In the Mosaic hypothesis of creation," Haeckel writes, "two great and fundamental ideas meet us with surprising clearness and simplicity." More still, I would add: "the Mosaic hypothesis of creation" answers the question of *where we come from,* which the theory of evolution will never do.[8] For that matter, neither anthropology, nor ethnography, nor linguistics will ever clarify *what we are.* Will they claim they never promised to do so? Nothing would be easier than to show that this was their sole objective. "I am convinced," Renan declared,

> that there is a science of the origins of mankind, and that it will be constructed one day not by abstract speculation *but by scientific research.* What human life in the actual condition of science would suffice to explore all the sides of this single problem? ... And if it be not resolved *how can we say that we know man and mankind?*[9]

Today, we may be quite certain the natural sciences will not tell us this. They might teach us what we are as animals! They will not teach us what we are as human beings. What is the origin of language? What is the origin of morality? All who have attempted to explain it in this century have failed miserably — and whoever tries will always fail, and just as miserably, for want of ability to conceive man without morality, without language, or outside of society. The very elements defining mankind elude the jurisdiction, the methods, and, finally, the grasp of science. Need I add that, all the more, the natural sciences will not resolve the question of *where we are going?* What has anatomy, what has physiology, taught us of our destiny? Yet they promised to explain it to us, to reveal our nature; from knowing our nature, knowledge of our destiny was then supposed to follow. Indeed, the destiny of a being determines its true nature.[10] Yet all their research and discoveries — whose interest I acknowledge, I might add — have wound up, in the end, only strengthening what attaches us to life; truth be told, this seems the height of unreason for a creature that must die.

Have the philological sciences kept their promises any better? Alas! At this very moment, I have before me all those books, famous not too long ago, where we sought answers to our doubts. But what, all in all, did they establish? The classicists formally vowed to show us the whole of Christianity in Greek and Roman philosophy! They forgot just one thing:

to say why, if Hellenistic culture already contained Christianity in its entirety, it did not emerge from this source. Yet that's the whole question. Even if the "scattered limbs" of the Sermon on the Mount were uncovered, one after the other, in Marcus Aurelius's *Meditations* or Epictetus's *Manual* — and even if the Stoic inspiration, which was essentially aristocratic, were not, in truth, opposite in spirit to the Gospels — the fact would remain that the Sermon on the Mount conquered the world, and that neither the *Manual* nor the *Meditations* engendered anything at all. Even after the labors of our classical scholars, there remains, as before, something in Christianity that they cannot explain: a singular virtue, a unique power of propagation and life — which the work of Hebraists confirms.[11]

The Hebraists also promised to dispel the "irrational" and "marvelous" from the history of Christianity and that of the "people of God." They were supposed to show us in the Bible a book like any other — the Semitic *Mahabharata*, the *Iliad* or *Odyssey* of Israel. Yet to this day, philologists haven't managed to assign a sure date of origin to either the *Odyssey* or the *Mahabharata*! Especially when facing the Bible, their systems — as varied as they are arbitrary — collide with each other. Seeking in vain to reconcile them under a law of indifference approaching skepticism, they have been forced to admit that their erudition obscures what it would illuminate. Consequently, there are some six or seven opinions concerning the origin and author of the Pentateuch. One may, if one so pleases, date its composition to the time of Joshua, for instance, or Saul or David or Solomon — or Josiah, or the Babylonian captivity, Ezra, the first Ptolemies, or the Maccabees, for that matter. The masters of modern philology will supply whatever justification one desires. Consider, too, how many theories there are about the date and the author of the fourth Gospel! If, in the end, one asks what this orgy of criticism has yielded, Bossuet's forceful words invariably come to mind:

> Tell me if it is not allowed, that from all the versions, and from any text whatever, there will still result the same laws, the same miracles, the same predictions, the same course of history, *the same body of doctrine, and in short the same substance?*[12]

He is right! It's the same substance, the same "course of history" — a unique history, as Renan himself confesses. An irreducible history! Whatever it may be, something in the history of the "people of God" is not found in the history of any other people. All efforts to "lower" it to the level of others, so to speak, it has resisted; indeed, it has emerged victorious. If exegesis, by an unforeseen detour, were one day to find confirmed what it claims to have destroyed, there would be no cause to marvel: this, after all, represents its sole hope for salvation today.[13] Until then, all one can say is that, far from having driven the "irrational" or the "wondrous" from the history of Christianity, exegesis has reintegrated them. Even in the history of Buddhism, the evolutionary analogies it pretends to have uncovered have not held up to more attentive and thorough examination.

That is still another promise — which the Orientalists, for their part, have failed to keep! The handful of resemblances between Buddhism and Christianity that have been detected, although they are infinitely curious, cannot, in fact, mask the profound difference, the core difference, which separates and indeed opposes them. I confess that, as science stands today, this difference is more a matter of feeling than definition. But if any of our Orientalists had possessed more open-mindedness or broader intellectual horizons, they would not have limited themselves to the scrupulous examination of texts; it is they who would have emerged as Christianity's most dangerous challengers. One day, they may be! But until then — like the Hebraists and the Hellenists — they will only have added, and in third place at that, an element of murkiness to the discussion: more reasons to doubt rather than believe, and preliminary hypotheses instead of solutions. Have they not occasionally claimed that Shakyamuni amounts to nothing but a "solar myth"? Were they to succeed in demonstrating as much some day, what would be left of the comparison so often made between Jesus Christ and Buddha?

Finally, the historical sciences — assuming they deserve this name at all. As with the natural sciences, I cannot deny that they have taught us many things, yet none of it is what one expected of their advances. For instance: did the kings of Rome exist, or are they also "solar myths"? That, no doubt, is what's called a "good question." Still, in all honesty, what does it matter to us? What is its inherent interest? The big question is whether a *law of history* exists and the extent to which we are subject to it. That, however, is precisely what we do not know. Indeed, I fear: it's what we'll never know. Are we our own masters, or are we the slaves of some *force majeure*? Does our path lead to a clear goal, or is history simply the "site," as it were, of incoherence and disorder? Neither paleography, nor the study of diplomacy, nor archeology has provided an answer. And yet these

fields owe us one if — as Renan puts it — we invent-
ed them in order to build a science of the "products of
the human spirit." This hold even if the sole purpose
of such a science were to augment, to specify, or to
"theorize" our knowledge of humanity.

> When a man writes upon the rulers of
> Nineveh or upon the Pharaohs of Egypt, he
> can only take a historical interest; but Christi-
> anity is such a living thing, and the problems
> of its origins involves such consequences for
> the most immediate present, that critics who
> would bring only historical interest to these
> questions are to be pitied for their imbecility.

These are the words of J.-F. Strauss.[14] For my part,
I would add that even when writing about the "Pha-
raohs of Egypt" or the "rulers of Nineveh," another
obligation holds — a higher one, and no less rigor-
ous: to establish the succession of shepherd kings, or
to describe with precision the palace of Khorsabad.
And if this is the very duty that, for the last fifty or
sixty years, the historical sciences have sought to escape, they should not be surprised to hear themselves
faulted for it. Zend and Assyrian were not created
to be taught from a pulpit at the Collège de France
or the University of Berlin; erudition cannot make itself its object; and just as juridical studies cannot be

separated from the philosophy of law, historical studies amount to nothing but vain curiosity if even their most modest efforts do not aim for the philosophy of history.

If the preceding does not represent complete "bankruptcy," at least it stands as so many "failures," and it is easy to see how they have damaged the credit of science. Who was so bold as to make the imprudent declaration "that science is of merit only to the extent that it can investigate what religion pretends to teach" — or, more still, "that science truly began only on that day when reason took itself seriously and said: 'I want for everything; I alone can assure my salvation'"? "Silence, imbecilic reason!" Pascal would surely have replied. True, we cannot say how matters will stand in a hundred years — much less a thousand years, or two thousand, from now. Still, for the moment — and for quite some time yet — it seems that reason cannot even free itself from its own doubts, much less assure its deliverance. And if it's true that science has sought to replace "religion" for the last hundred years, then science has lost the match — both for the time being and for the foreseeable future. Unable to provide even an initial response to the sole questions of interest, neither science in general nor the individual disciplines — physics, the study of nature, philology, or history — is entitled to what they have claimed for a century: to govern life in the present. Failing absolute certainty, mathematical and thought-through, when we need to fashion an idea of what we are — and if the social bond can only hold on this condition — the sciences may help us, but they have no right to define, much less judge, this idea. For the moment, with science as it stands — after what we have experienced of it — the question of free will, for example, or of moral responsibility, cannot be made a matter of physiology. The progress claimed by Taine and those who have followed him, which was supposed to "fuse" — as he put it himself — "the moral sciences and the natural sciences," yielded no progress at all; on the contrary, it was a move backward. Were we to ask Darwinism to guide our conduct, its lessons would be simply abominable.[15] Needless to say, a Darwinism scarcely sure of its principles, or a physiology which is even more primitive, allows for appeals to a more advanced physiology or more sophisticated Darwinism. But in the meanwhile, we must live, and live a life that is not purely animal — and no science, no science today, can give us the means to do so.

This is the reason for the revolution — or the evolution —we are now witnessing. If need be, one could find ample proof in the *Bibliographie de la France*. I harbor no illusions about the *Decadents of Christianity* — the title of another book that fails to deliver what it promises — nor would I willingly leave philology and exegesis even to "neo-Catholics" or our "symbolists." If sincere ones number in their ranks, I know of others who are less so and ultimately believe only in themselves. I have still less faith in "neo-Buddhists" and their routines, and none at all in those new "mystics" one can see relaxing with a translation of Tauler or Ruysbroeck while writing a play for the Théâtre-Libre. Twenty years ago, I'm quite sure, they would have been naturalists: their mystical airs are nothing but fashion or "advertising" for their publishers. Finally, I don't attach undue significance to the pious declamations one is sometimes surprised to discover in *Le Peuple français* or *L'Autorité*.... Yet all the same, a development is now in course, and we are already beginning to see some of its effects.[16] Two words are all it takes to sum them up: Science has lost its prestige, and Religion has regained a share of its former status.

II

"All religious reaction redounding to the immediate benefit of Catholicism"— Renan himself says so — it's not surprising that a politically-minded pope, inspired by the foremost necessity of the hour at hand, has conceived the hope and articulated the project for directing the movement. He has every right to do so. *Multae sunt mansiones in domo patris mei:* there are multiple aspects, or several faces, of Christianity, as it were. Formerly, when times were strange and confusing, the Church triumphed over such eruptions and revolts of nature — surely one of the defining characteristics of the Renaissance. It even wrested the empire of art from fifteenth-century paganism. Some hundred and fifty or two hundred years later, it managed to pose a counterweight to the formidable influence of Cartesianism by absorbing it — and even making use of it to develop the rational substance of its own teachings. Finally, at the outset of the century now in course, the Church did not refuse to have truck with the Revolution, and it managed to do so without abandoning its rights or surrendering its dogma. Why, then, in a time such as our own, if its tradition offers something of social virtue and no regard for temporal order hinders its free development, would it not endeavor to show itself to the nations in its new aspect? Why, moreover, should it not succeed? Evolving does not mean changing, an ancient Father declared. *Quod evolvitur... non ideo proprietate mutatur.* These are the very words of Saint Vincent of Lerins. The blossoming of a tree's leaves is not a "variation" of the seed. Nor is it "change," a becoming-different, to develop the implications of a law once it is made. On the contrary, this brings the process of self-becoming to completion.[17] The Church never forgot this, but other, more pressing worries — notably, to withstand and counter the assault of lay science — preoccupied Leo XIII's predecessors. As times change, so, too, do the challenges! Who, today, would abandon the Church's communion for "philological reasons"? What's more, if it is now clear that physical, or natural, science is powerless to dispel "mystery," let us again return to the source. May the spirit of peace and reconciliation prevail. Free and liberated from the demands of struggle that have been consuming our forces, we should not prolong bootless controversy. Having proven the truth, or the "divinity," of religion by way of immutable dogma, let us now prove the same on the basis of the good it may yet do for our turbulent and troubled world.

That, more or less, is how one may picture the intentions of Pope Leo XIII. Indeed, it seems that for seventeen years, all his words and deeds have sought to realize this grand design. The pontiff who wrote the memorable encyclical of 28 December 1878, *On Modern Errors*, that of 11 August 1879, *On Christian Philosophy*, and that of 10 February 1880, *On Chris-*

tian Marriage, in no way surrendered the Church's rights or the authority of its dogma — even though the second scandalized all those who learned, evidently for the first time, that Saint Thomas stands as one of the most sublime intellects to have illustrated the history of human thought. In proclaiming the Church's independence with respect to forms of government, in addressing questions of labor with particular scrupulousness, and in working toward the future reconciliation of the various Christian communions, Leo XIII performed three great things. The first is to have given Catholicism, and religion in general, a share in social action. "Catholics," he wrote in his *Encyclical on the Origin of Civil Power,* 29 June 1881,

> affirm that the right to rule is from God, as from a natural and necessary principle. It is of importance, however, to remark in this place that those who may be placed over the State may in certain cases be chosen by the will and decision of the multitude, *judicio multitudinis*, without opposition to or impugning the Catholic doctrine, *non adversante neque repugnante doctrina catholica....* There is no question here respecting forms of government, for there is no reason why the Church should not approve of the chief pow-

er being held by one man or more, provided only it be just, and that it tend to the common advantage. Wherefore ... the people are not hindered from choosing for themselves that form of government which suits best either their own disposition, or the institutions and customs of their ancestors.

These words are abundantly clear! Yet thoughts mature slowly in Leo XIII's mind, which is what confers such gravity and authority on all he says. Accordingly, he has seen fit to take up this weighty question on several occasions. In his *Letter to the French Cardinals,* of May 3, 1892, one reads:

This, too, we explained, *and we desire to restate it* that no one may be in doubt as to our meaning. One way [of achieving unity] is to accept without reserve, with that perfect loyalty beseeming a Christian, the civil power in the form in which it *de facto* exists. Thus the first Empire was accepted in France on the morrow of frightful and bloody anarchy. Thus were accepted the other successive powers, whether monarchic or Republican, down to our own time.

... When, therefore, in a society a constituted
and active power exists, common interest
must be allied to that power, and for this reason it should be accepted as it is. It is for this
reason and with this intent that we told the
French Catholics: "Accept the Republic, that
is to say, the constituted power in your midst,
respect it, be submissive to it as representing
the power come from God."

His language was no less clear, and no less con-
ciliatory, on the question of labor. In the encyclical
issued on 29 June 1881, he addressed the disquiet that
besieges modern societies and struck a bold tone:

This, indeed, is all the graver because rulers,
in the midst of such threatening dangers, have
no remedies sufficient to restore discipline
and tranquility. They supply themselves with
the power of laws, and think to coerce, by
the severity of their punishment, those who
disturb their governments. They are right
to a certain extent, but yet they should seriously consider that no power of punishment
can be so great that it alone can preserve the
State: *vim nullam poenarum futuram quae
conservare respublicas sola possit.* For fear,
as St. Thomas admirably teaches, "is a weak

foundation; for those who are subdued by
fear would, should an occasion arise in which
they might hope for immunity, rise more
eagerly against their rulers, in proportion to
the previous extent of their restraint through
fear." And what is more, "from too great
fear many fall into despair; despair inspires
boldness; and boldness precipitates the most
monstrous of crimes."

Although the remedy lies in returning to Christian
principles, these principles have immediate and practical applications. The Pope foregrounded them in the
celebrated encyclical of 15 May 1891, *Rights and Duties of Capital and Labor:*

As regards the State, the interests of all,
whether high or low, are equal. The members
of the working classes are citizens by nature
and by the same right as the rich; they are
real parts, living the life which makes up,
through the family, the body of the common-
wealth; and it need hardly be said that they
are in every city very largely the majority.
It would be irrational to neglect one portion
of the citizens and favor another, and therefore the public administration must duly and

solicitously provide for the welfare and the comfort of the working classes....

If we turn to matters which are not external and material, the first thing of all is to save unfortunate workers from the cruelty of speculators who, making no distinction between human beings and machines, abuse their persons beyond measure to satisfy their own insatiable greed. To demand an amount of work that, blunting all spiritual faculties, crushes the body and consumes its forces entirely, is conduct that neither justice nor humanity can tolerate.

The result of civil change and revolution has been to divide cities into two classes separated by a wide chasm. On the one side stands the party which holds power because it holds wealth; which has in its grasp the whole of labor and trade; which manipulates for its own benefit and its own purposes all the sources of supply.... On the other side stands the needy and powerless multitude, sick and sore in spirit and ever ready for disturbance. If working people can be encouraged to look forward to obtaining a share in the land, the consequence will be that the gulf between vast wealth and sheer poverty will be bridged, and the respective classes will be brought nearer to one another.

The *Letter on the Labor Question* — written to M. G. Decurtins on 7 August 1893 — is also relevant:

If there are grounds grave and just for which the public authority may intervene to protect by law the weak condition of laborers, certainly none is graver or more just than the necessity to assist children and women.

Moreover, it is evident how imperfect the protection granted workers would be, were it made by various laws established by each people for its own account; for inasmuch as different goods from diverse countries meet on the same market, it is certain that different regulations imposed on labor here and there would entail the consequence that the products of one nation's industry prove detrimental to another's.

Even as he was writing these words, Leo XIII had surely conceived an even bolder idea. His vigorous imagination had already discerned the horizon evident in the encyclical of 20 June 1894, *The Reunion of Christendom*:

With these thoughts in mind — the reconciliation of the Protestant and Eastern Churches
with the Church of Rome — and appealing
with our most heartfelt prayers to achieve
the same, we see, in the distant future, a new
order of things unfolding upon the earth;
nothing could be sweeter than to contemplate
the benefits that would naturally result. It can
hardly be imagined what immediate and rapid
progress would occur among all nations: the
establishment of tranquility and peace; the
promotion of art and learning; and, between
the cultivators of the soil, workmen, and
industrialists, the founding, on the Christian
principles we have indicated, of new societies
able to repress usury and enlarge the field of
useful labor: *quarum ope vorax reprimatur
usura, et utilium laborum campus dilate-
tur.*

Another passage declares:

We are well aware of the long and tiresome
labors involved in the restoration of the order
we desire; and there may be many who think
that we are far too sanguine and looking for
things to be wished for more than expected.... However, we appeal to princes and

rulers, in the name of their statesmanship
and solicitude for their peoples, to weigh our
counsels in the balance of truth and second
them with their authority.... The past century
has left Europe worn out from disasters, still
trembling from the turmoil that convulsed it.
Why, in turn, should the present century, now
hastening to a close, not bequeath pledges of
concord to mankind as its legacy, with the
prospect of great benefits promised by the
unity of the Christian Faith?

These lines' nobility is matched only by the sincerity of the emotion animating them. To be sure, no dream — if the Holy Father's own mode of expression permits us to use the word — and no hope better suits either the aspirations at the end of this century or the character of the illustrious and venerable man who governs, with nearly full sovereignty, the faith of two hundred million human beings. Leo XIII has understood what is expected of mankind's greatest, and most ancient, moral authority. With resolute hand, he launched St. Peter's vessel on the stormy seas of the age; neither the gusting winds, nor the roiling waves, nor even the shouts and calls of passengers frightened by his tranquil courage have swayed his course for even a single day. And if the goal has not been achieved — if Providence, whose instrument he knows himself to be, has not yet permitted him to reach the destination — he has the imperishable honor of having charted the way on his own.

The future will surely thank him for remembering that Christianity started out as a religion of the poor — that, as Voltaire remarked with such insolence and cruelty, "only the lowest rabble welcomed it for more than a hundred years." I fear Renan wanted to say the very same — more elegantly, but less candidly — when he urged us not to picture the voyages of Paul and Barnabas as those "of a Livingstone... or François Xavier"; instead, he averred, they were "like those of socialist workers propagating their ideas from cabaret to cabaret." No doubt, he commended himself for having found this turn of phrase! *Differantur isti superbi, aliqua soliditate sanandi sunt.* The Gospel does not turn away the great, the mighty, or the wise. It does not reject them, yet it does "set them apart." That is the glory of Christianity, what provided its vigor when it first began. Perhaps there is no sign more striking or proof more convincing of its mission than the fact that it started by addressing the humble of this world. Therein lies its future, too — and, so to speak, the promise of eternity even within the society the last century's philosophy has made.[18] No pontiff has ever felt it more clearly than Pope Leo XIII, nor, having sensed as much, declared it with greater magnanimity or persuasive ardor. No one has reaffirmed it so insistently. And certainly no one — in telling both those who are grieved by useless violence and revolt, as well as those who enjoy the good fortune of the day, how duties to their "brethren" override all others — has done so with a fuller sense of human fraternity, Christian equality, or apostolic liberty.

III

In the meanwhile, what are we to do? Clearly, we will not sacrifice science, much less our independence of thought. If we do not grant that science can ever replace religion — and I believe I have said as much with sufficient frankness — we also refuse to admit that religion be set in opposition to science. Nor does the Church ask this of anyone. Why should it? As we have seen, the Haeckels and Renans of the world[19] are those who have recognized, in the biblical narrative of creation, for example, the purest spirit of evolutionary doctrine. I would add that science's radical inability to resolve questions of first and final things seems to have brought about a separation between the domain of "scientific" certainty and that of "inspired" certainty. And so it may stand as duly established: physics can offer nothing to explain the miraculous, whose definition is that nature makes an exception to its own laws; exegesis has nothing to offer when faced with revelation[20]; and finally, I make bold to declare, if ever a purely secular morality is founded — one independent of all religion (which is not to say independent of all metaphysics) — it will not be based on physiology. Our independence of thought, then, will suffer only to the extent that faith proves a matter of experience and reasoning. But that's just it: faith is neither a matter of reasoning nor of experience. The divinity of the Christ is not to be demonstrated. It is either affirmed or denied. Either one believes, or one does not — as holds for the immortality of the soul, as holds for the existence of God.[21] That is why, as I have said, if one takes a calm look at the issue, we have nothing to lose. It is not science's place to undermine or strengthen "proofs of religion"; nor is it incumbent upon religion to deny or evaluate the laws of gravity or the facts established by Egyptologists. Each endeavor has its own, separate realm. And because it is not up to us to make ourselves the subjects of either the one or the other, or of both at once, what more can one ask for?

For all that, is it possible for us to separate "morality" from religion in the same fashion? That is a different question — one far weightier and more delicate.

Indeed, it seems that morality has not been tied to religion everywhere and at all times. One might rightly claim that in classical antiquity, Stoicism, among other doctrines, or even Epicureanism, "posed" itself only by "opposing" the practices and superstitions of paganism. Socrates, to be sure, was an atheist as far as Aristophanes's "gods" were concerned.[22] On the other hand, the claim has been advanced that religion created morality. At this very moment, a book lies before me: *La Religion basée sur la morale.* The volume collects lectures delivered in America and England a few years ago. If I have understood properly, the general aim is to affirm that man finds God only by seeking Him within. But as different as they seem, all the opinions make the same point when they affirm that morality represents the invention or achievement of mankind. In my opinion, Edmond Scherer proved more farsighted in a remarkable article he wrote in 1884, *Crise actuelle de la morale:*

> Let us view matters as they really are: morality — the true, the good, the ancient, and the imperative one — *needs the absolute*; it aspires to transcendence; it finds its stay only in God…. Conscience is like the heart: it needs a beyond. Duty is nothing if it is not

sublime, and life becomes frivolous if not
tied by eternal bonds.[23]

That is the real way to pose the problem, and perhaps to resolve it. In fact, it does not matter whether
morality came from religion, or religion from morality — nor even that there have been "immoral"
religions or moralities "without God." I affirm the
same apropos of the question whether a purely secular
morality, as discussed above, will one day be instituted. It is not yet time. The first question — concerning the "supernatural" component of morality, or the
moral component of the "religion" observed by Numa
Pompilius's contemporaries — is idle for the time being inasmuch as it interests only historians. But what
is key, what is certain, is that morality and religion do
not assume their full meaning — they do not fulfill the
whole of their definition, so to speak — except by suffusing one another and, if I dare put it this way, amalgamating. "Morality is nothing if it is not religious,"
to quote Scherer again; and what would remain of a
religion if one removed morality from it?

One way to prove as much would be to show that,
for almost two thousand years now — and up into the
present century — all efforts to secularize morality
have never provided anything but a deformation, alteration, or disguised version of a "Christian" idea.

Bayle, in the past, and Taine, in our own day, sought to base it on man's natural perversity, that is, on the need to check, subdue, or eliminate the impulses within us that arise from animal instinct. This is a Christian idea — indeed, it is the dogma of "original sin." A wonderful page of *Elevations on the Mysteries*, so literal and symbolic at once, makes it plain:

> Let us restrain the lively starts of our wandering thoughts.... We will command, in some way, the birds of the sky; let us keep our thoughts from always crawling among bodily needs, as do the reptiles upon the earth.... Mastering our impetuous rage will be the taming of lions. We will subdue venomous animals when we know to quell hatred, jealousy, and calumny. We will bridle a fiery steed when we check our pleasures.

Likewise, one finds a Christian notion — grace — in all forms of mystical morality. Another, absolute justice occurs in all systems of morality founded, like Kant's, on "the autonomy of will." To be sure, positivist morality exists — one founded on the idea of commiseration, the solidarity of interests that tie one person to the next in the infinite extension of space and time, down through the generations of man. George Eliot has lent it its noblest expression:

May I reach

That purest heaven, be to other souls

The cup of strength in some great agony,

Enkindle generous ardor, feed pure love,

Beget the smiles that have no cruelty —

Be the sweet presence of a good diffused,

And in diffusion ever more intense.[24]

Yet who cannot recognize here the very idea of *Catholicism* — or, more precisely, of *Catholicity* — combined with the idea of virtuous sacrifice? So greatly are we suffused with Christianity! *In eo vivimus, movemur et sumus.* If ever we should reject it, it would be the greatest event in the history of the world — after that of its institution![25]

For those who do not think that a democracy can fail to show interest in morality — who know, moreover, that one does not govern men against a force as formidable as religion — it is simply a matter of choosing, among the different forms of Christianity, the one best suited to regenerating morals. Without hesitation, I affirm this to be Catholicism.

I would not omit the considerable merits of Protestantism in this regard, its historical reason for existence, or the examples of virtue it has provided and continues to provide every day.[26] All the same, Catholicism possesses great advantages, the first of which — as Renan puts it — is to be "the most apparent and the most religious of all religions." Catholicism is a government, whereas Protestantism is simply the absence of government. As much is proven by its history, which, properly speaking, consists solely of its many divisions. Imagine an army whose soldiers refused to obey their officers because they held different opinions about discipline and duty: that is the very picture of Protestantism. "Place Ignatius Loyola at Oxford," it has been said — and I needn't add it was a Protestant who did so —

> he is certain to become the head of a formidable secession. Place John Wesley at Rome. He is certain to be the first general of a new society devoted to the interest and honour of the Church. Place St. Theresa in London. Her restless enthusiasm ferments into madness, not untinctured with craft. Place Joanna Southcote at Rome. She founds an order of barefooted Carmelites, every one of whom is ready to suffer martyrdom for the Church.[27]

In other words: for want of constituting a government, Protestantism, which is conventionally admired for its flexibility, loses its slightest heretics forever. In contrast, Catholicism, whose "plasticity" has so often escaped notice, regularly absorbs, annuls, and sometimes manages to use its heretics — because it is a government. Is it not a great advantage, when ruling men, to start out by actually being a government?[28]

As a government, Catholicism also constitutes a "doctrine" and a "tradition," whose full force I have come to appreciate in reading Tolstoy's most recent essay, *Christianity and Patriotism.* I marveled at how wise — and politically astute, moreover — Catholicism has been in always refusing to hand Scripture over to individual interpretation. For it is written: "If any man come to me, and hate not his father, and mother, and wife, and children, and brethren, and sisters, yea, and his own life also, he cannot be my disciple." Yes, that is written! And elsewhere: "And again I say unto you, it is easier for a camel to go through the eye of a needle, than for a rich man to enter into the kingdom of God." Needless to say, if the spirit of tradition does not flow into the letter of the text, what effect will such words produce in a humble reader — *infimae sortis, pauperculae domus* — for they have led even the greatest contemporary Russian

author astray in a labyrinth of error! I now understand what was meant, in the past, when the quarrel
between Protestants and Catholics was boiled down
to "Church matters." The very notion — as it were,
the concept — of Holy Writ or the Book cannot be
separated from instituting an authority to explain
it. " But how!" Saint Augustine already exclaimed,
"whereas there is no science or art so simple it does
not require a guide and master, only religion, among
all the things of the world, should need no teaching or
direction?" Is a greater contradiction even possible?
Who can fail to see that, if Scripture in itself were sufficiently transparent to all minds, it would offer nothing surpassing the lights of mankind, and we would
have no need for a God to "reveal" it to us? And if
"revelation" were complete — if it did not need to be
perpetually illuminated as if from above — we would
be God Himself. Protestantism surely has "reason"
on its side, yet religion is not philosophy; one must
acknowledge that "logic" speaks for Catholicism.

Finally, Catholicism is more than just "theology"
or "psychology." If I may be so bold, it must also
provide "sociology." And there, let it be known, at
the critical hour we are now facing, lies its greatest
advantage. Just try to define the essence of Protestantism: its greatest concern is individual salvation.

The sinner grows confused, suffers injury, and, to speak with Luther's words, is engulfed by conscience of his unworthiness, terror before his Judge, and fear of damnation. "The slightest failings seem crimes to him," for he has neither "indulgences" nor "works" to make amends. Indeed, preoccupation with faith destroys hope in his heart; and when hope founders, in turn charity sinks.[29]

Indeed, how can one show concern for others when one is worried about oneself to this degree — and all the more so because conscience proves more exacting and fierce?[30] However monstrously the doctrine of indulgences and works may occasionally have been abused, it is enough to take Catholicism back its first principles to recognize their social fecundity. The merits of the ones "apply" to the salvation of the others. The barefooted Carmelite in his cloister weeping for the sins of the worldly effaces their trespasses. The monk who goes about begging on the roads redeems the adulterous woman through the humiliation he endures. And so, perpetual charity circulates in Catholic society, in its ideal form. The living pray for the dead, and the dead intercede for the living. A more clement justice, a God more kindly disposed to human weakness accords the grace of the elect to the outcast. And from the center to the circumference of this infinite circle, which encompasses the whole of humanity, there is no one whom others' sins do not distress, but also no one whom others' merits do not console....

Does this mean we can expect of "Catholicism," or of "religion" in general, what we have been waiting for in vain from science for three or four hundred years? We cannot, to be sure, except to the extent that we have "faith" — the one thing one cannot simply give oneself at will. But as for all worldly affairs, just as there are times to speak, there are times to be silent; and for the moment, I fail to see what might be objected to Catholic doctrine on the separation of the "moral sciences" and "natural sciences." That, as is well known, was Taine's delusion: to "weld" the one to the other; and nothing is more forced — indeed, sad, in a sense — in his final works than his efforts to persuade himself that he had succeeded. Even if all our instincts were of purely animal origin — a matter, incidentally, one need not admit — these instincts would still have proven strangely different from themselves for the six thousand years that civilization has sought to wrest us from servitude to nature. Spinoza notwithstanding, we would still have made of them an "empire within an empire." As the condition of mankind, this new form of determinism — moral determinism — would have nothing in common with all that "conditions" the phenomena investigated by the physical and natural sciences. In the past, official spirituality — that of Cousin and Jouffroy — was faulted for seeking to place morality everywhere, and at any price. Contemporary positivism has yielded to excess in the opposite sense, by pretending to treat morality as it does physiology; in so doing, it has shot just as wide from the true mark. There is nothing that warrants the confusion it engineered by making morals dependent on knowledge. This is the first point where we must agree with the teachings of the Church — nor need I demonstrate its import.

And here is another. Perhaps the gravest philosophical error of the last century — which Diderot exemplified at least as much as, or more than, Rousseau — was to have substituted the dogma of natural human goodness for that of innate perversity. Here and elsewhere, I have endeavored to show what a skeptic like Bayle — whom no one will accuse of intellectual timidity — called "the necessity of a principle of repression." If nature is immoral, this holds within us just as much as it does in the outside world. Believing as much with absolute conviction, how could one be surprised or shocked by the words of the encyclical *Humanum Genus:*

human nature was stained by original sin,
and is therefore more disposed to vice than to
virtue. For a virtuous life it is absolutely necessary to restrain the disorderly movements
of the soul, and to make the passions obedi-
ent to reason.... But the naturalists deny that
our first parents sinned, and consequently
think that free will is not at all weakened and
inclined to evil. On the contrary, exaggerating
rather the power and the excellence of nature,
and placing therein alone the principle and
rule of justice, they cannot even imagine that
there is any need at all of a constant struggle
and a perfect steadfastness to overcome the
violence and rule of our passions.

These words are the very truth. Acknowledging as
much does not make one either Protestant or Catholic;
one may even be an evolutionist. Indeed! Evolution-
ists, in particular, are unable to picture human nature
any other way. Don't they consider the blood in our
veins to be the same as what flowed, in prehistoric
times, in the veins of our primal ancestors — a kind of
fire fuelling lubricious and ferocious instincts? If orthodox apologetics surely has its reasons not to have
made more of this argument, some advocates of the
idea of evolution — including myself — have been

won over, in part, by this very claim.[31] This is the second point of agreement: virtue is nothing other than the will's victory over nature. In other words, and without any metaphor: will does not achieve determination except by freeing itself from nature.

Just as readily, one may grant that the "social question" is simply a "moral question." This is also the title a German philosopher gave one of his books not too long ago — and it would represent an immense gain if its full significance were appreciated: *The Social Question, A Moral Question.*[32] In effect, this means that however much one may pretend that such a thing does not exist, no scientific measures will ever eliminate unequal conditions among human beings. Then again, should one hope for anything of the kind?[33] There will always be, as there are now, those who are stronger. But there will always be, as there have always been, ways to lessen the consequences of inequality that trouble the mind even more than they weigh on the heart. It means that the "social contract" is not an insurance contract; consequently, no one should seek to shift the burden of his duty toward his fellow man onto an anonymous power, nor should anyone profit from the advantages of society without acquitting himself of the costs involved. Finally, it means that, besides obligations *not-to,* there are obligations to act within us; foremost among them is to endeavor to destroy the root of egoism, our animal attachment to life…. Yet the "social question" does not stand at issue here. I deem it enough to have indicated what is implied when one poses it as a moral issue. After all, the implications are clear: to seek a solution in the analogies offered by natural history, as our sociologists do, or in the tyrannical extension of state power, as the socialists do, or in the destruction of all society, like the anarchists, is to follow an illusion — yet one may only approach it by making demands of individual morality!

The conclusion is plain. When agreement prevails on three or four points of this magnitude, there is no need to discuss conditions or terms. An understanding has been reached. It would amount to a kind of crime if the good will of several generations were not appealed to and obtained, such that these three or four points come to stand beyond all doubt; at any rate, it would be the most unpardonable folly to try to pit such good intentions against each other, or divide them on grounds of interpretation and geography. Even supposing that social progress occurs at the price of temporary sacrifice — which would cost our independence and dignity nothing, but surely our vanity — there can be no hesitation. After all, one must live, and life is not a matter of contemplation or speculating so much as acting. A sick man scoffs at the rules, provided he be cured. When a house is burning, its occupants' sole concern is to extinguish the flames. Finally, to offer a comparison that is nobler, and perhaps truer, as well: there is no time to set individual caprice in opposition to the rights of the community — when battle looms.[34]

NOTES.

i Antoine Compagnon, *Connaissez-vous Brunetière? Enquête sur un antidreyfusard et ses amis* (Paris: Seuil, 1997). [EB]

ii For a lively account of the author's life and fortunes, see Elton Hocking, *Ferdinand Brunetière: The Evolution of a Critic* (Madison: University of Wisconsin Press, 1936). [EB]

iii E.g., Jean Baudrillard, *Fatal Strategies*, trans. Phil Beitchman (Los Angeles: Semiotext[e], 2008), 23, where he describes "monstrous conformity to empty space, ... deformity by excess of conformity.... This strange obesity is no longer that of a protective layer of fat nor the neurotic one of depression. It is neither the compensatory obesity of the underdeveloped nor the alimentary one of the overnourished. Paradoxically, it is a mode of disappearance for the body. The secret rule that delimits the sphere of the body has disappeared. The secret form of the mirror, by which the body watches over itself and its image, is abolished, yielding to the unrestrained redundancy of a living organism. No more limits, no more transcendence: it is as if the body were no longer opposed to an external world, but sought to digest space in its own appearance." [EB] ⁱᵛ Cf. Byung-Chul Han, *The Transparency Society,* trans. Erik Butler (Stanford: Stanford University Press, 2015), 1-8. [EB]

ᵛ Evidently, a "dislike" feature is in the course of development; significantly, however, it will not express disapproval so much as commiseration: "disliking" news of a breakup or death, for instance. [EB]

NOTES ON THE TEXT

ⁱ Although I thought this declaration was sufficiently categorical, it hasn't been taken as such. In particular, my rejection, from the outset, of all accusations of *reportage* has led to the conclusion that I merited them. That's how people reason today! A French delegate, M. Vigné d'Octon, who was abroad in Italy at the time, even got it into his head to request his own audience with the Pope, to ask His Holiness what He thought of how I had represented His ideas. I hardly merit such honor! There's nothing left for me now but make my way to Rome and the Vatican once more to interrogate the Holy Father about the fidelity of M. Vigné d'Octon's recollections. But because I have already stated as much, I prefer simply to say it again: *not a word*, in the pages that follow, refers to the conversation the Holy Father was kind enough

to grant me; and whatever one thinks of the ideas
I express, it is my concern, duty, and pleasure to
claim full responsibility for them.

2 That is what the young Renan — when he was
only the author of *Studies of Religious History
and even The Life of Jesus* — never failed to note
when possible; and Voltaire, in his day, was hardly
less odious than Béranger himself, with his *God
of Honest People!* But when Renan realized that,
on the whole, the conclusions he reached in *Origins of Christianity* closely resembled the opinions
of Voltaire, he changed his mind. That attests to
his loyalty, and, in his *History of the People of
Israel*, one sees him trade the contempt of old for
jokes of a rather low order, which is no credit to
his taste. Like the author of the *Bible Explained
by the Chaplains of the King of Poland*, he had as
much fun as he could at the expense of Yahweh, "a
creature of the narrowest spirit," and so he thought
he was working wonders when he likened David
to Troppmann. I like him better, as a man, when
he plays this role: at least he has the merit of being
more straightforward; however, I prefer him as an
author in the other capacity.

3 André Lefèvre, *La Religion,* pp. 572, 573.

4 To conceive an accurate notion of how much good
faith prevails in discussions and polemics today, I
consider it my duty to remark that I took care, on

this very page, to present all the objections voiced
in the name of science; all my opponents had to do
was develop them. Not only did I not deny scientific advances such as the "telephone" and "vaccine
for croup" — which would be as ridiculous as
denying the light of the sun at high noon — but I
said, word for word, "what promises have physics
or chemistry not kept — or surpassed?" Therefore,
those who responded with lengthy lists of scientific
advances taught me nothing I hadn't already said.
All they did was try to pull the wool over their
readers' eyes — and if they didn't fall for it themselves, I wonder what kind of discussion this is?
I'm hardly afraid of their response.

Equally, I foresaw, and warned of, the objection
that others have not failed to draw from the fact
that I am not a qualified "physicist" or "chemist."
All the same, it gave rise to whole articles!
Why, then, did I write: "if a member of our learned
society who's a bit fantastical or adventurous in
spirit has undertaken unapproved activities in the
name of science, is science itself to be accused?"
Too simple and naïve, I prided myself in anticipat-
ing the response others have now made by asking:
"What are the great names of science one could
place beneath these haughty manifestos for which
science itself is supposed to be responsible?" How
far off the mark I was! As the saying goes, there's
none more deaf than the man who will not listen. I

will return to this point shortly.

5 *Esquisse d'un tableau des progrès de l'esprit hu-
   main.* Édition Didot, t. IV des Oeuvres, p. 395.

6 *L'Avenir de la science*, p. 37.

7 This represents a key item of debate. I have been
   told that science never made the "promises" for
   which it is supposed to account — and neither
   "Encyclopedists" of the last century nor the "Hege-
   lians" of our own have any right to speak in its
   name. Let's take a look at this objection.

   1. I gladly allow that Renan is not a "scientist";
   indeed, I am happy to have obtained this important
   admission. After all, he had the pretension of prac-
   ticing science! If he prided himself on anything at
   all, it was to have introduced, to matters of exegesis
   and philology, rigor, precision, and methodological
   subtlety equal — or at least analogous — to those
   of physiology and chemistry themselves. This is as
   plain as day in the details of his style, where "pseu-
   doscientific" comparisons abound — and, what is
   graver still, provide the basis for conclusions that
   claim to be historical or moral. And so, yet again,
   I am not in the least grieved to see him stripped of
   the title. From this day forth, I publicly commit
   myself to seeing in him nothing more than a "liter-

ary professional" — an artist, poet, and dilettante. As for Condorcet, I am equally delighted, even though the question is a bit more delicate here. How, after all, could I forget that Jean-Antoine-Nicolas Caritat, marquis de Condorcet, was, in his day, the "Perpetual Secretary of the Academy of Sciences?" And where will it get us if we admit that one may be the "Perpetual Secretary of the Academy of Sciences" without being a "scientist" oneself?

2. It's important to try to be loyal. When mere philosophers, "literary professionals" like Auguste Comte — and, closer to our own times, men like Littré, Taine, and Renan himself (along with a good twenty others one might name) — claim adherence to science, does science refuse them? Has it pushed away the alliance they offered? Was the triumph of their ideas not science's own triumph as much as it was theirs? Science, then, has the right to go over their ideas with a fine-toothed comb, as it were, and retain only what it acknowledges as conforming to its own certainties. It has no right to repudiate its allies of old! It owes them at least a share in its prestige and "popularity." If, perhaps, they have spoken on its behalf with some imprudence, and without being fittingly authorized, science has still profited from their enthusiasm and talent. They are

the ones who have won others to its cause, not the inventors of gas lighting or the tubular boiler. If they haven't distinguished themselves through their own "scientific" discoveries, properly speaking, it is they who have assured that "science" holds sway over the present age. That is why, for the "promises" they have made in its name, science is now accountable to us: an honest man does not answer solely for business he has done, but also for what he has signed for!

3. This is also exactly what those who are truly learned do, and the words quoted in the article exempt me from adding any more. Those of M. Berthelot are enough — from "La Science et la Morale," which appeared in the *Revue de Paris* (1 February 1895). Here, and for the time being, I am not discussing the article's premise. Only the conclusion matters:

> We see every day how the application of
> scientific doctrines to industry increases
> the wealth and prosperity of nations....
> The application of the same doctrines
> diminishes suffering without cease... and
> increases the average span of life. Equal-
> ly, the history of this century proves the
> extent to which the fate of all has been
> improved by new ideas.... Such are the

results of the scientific method. *Thus the universal triumph of science will finally assure mankind the maximum of happiness and morality.*

Neither Condorcet nor Renan ever said anything more. All they promised, it is clear, another "Perpetual Secretary of the Academy of Sciences," is now promising in turn. What, after that, remains of the supposed "responses" which fault me for attributing to science ambitions that it never had?

8 I was surprised by M. Berthelot's unexpected response to this observation. "The mystic," he claims,

> who would presume to direct his life and private affairs *solely according to notions of the wondrous would soon be lost.* Both history and mental pathology show that nations and individuals who have adopted mystery and divine inspiration as fundamental guides have soon found themselves cast into material, intellectual, and moral ruin, and irreparably so.

Truly, one would like to know what "peoples" the sapient chemist has in mind! Did the Romans, Greeks, or Egyptians make divine inspiration and mystery their "fundamental guides"? And today, in the modern world, are Russia, England, or the United States of America — which are all much more concerned with religious questions than one is in France — faring the worse for it? What holds for individuals holds for "peoples": they die... because they are "mortal" and have had their day; fortunately, no one can live forever.

What, moreover, does "mental pathology" mean here? As far as I know, neither Bossuet nor Calvin died "mad" or "raving." Or could it be, perchance, that none may be sure of eluding "general paresis" except for "geometers and physicists"? That would be a singular privilege.

Finally, what does it mean to conduct one's life "solely according to notions of the wondrous," and for what readers did our sage think he was writing? The "wondrous" is not "mystery," and M. Berthelot couldn't care less! If "notions of the wondrous" exist — that is, if this expression signifies anything at all — "spiritists" might conduct their lives according to them, but "spiritism" and "spiritualism" are not the same. The more I reread the sentence, the less sense it offers. Surely it comes from "a stranger to the philosophical spirit." Moreover, I like to think that M. Berthelot usually brings greater precision and perspicacity to bear on "scientific questions."

9 *L'Avenir de la science*, p. 163.

10 A young professor of philosophy — whom I am calling young because he treats me as an old dodderer —kindly drew attention to this sentence in the *Revue de Métaphysique et de Morale* and asked whether it shouldn't be the other way around. But in stating that "the destiny of a being determines its true nature," I believe I said what I meant, and not the opposite; I'm a little astonished that a philosopher, who knows what a *final cause* is, did not understand right away. It is quite important, for instance, where human conduct is concerned, to know whether the object of this life is held by and, as it were, contained within the limits of one's current existence, or if, on the contrary, it exceeds them. This can effect morality as a whole! If we are utterly annihilated at death, many virtues remain — I would hardly disagree — yet we will not treat the instincts within us in the same manner. It follows that determining our true nature closely depends on knowledge of our destiny. If we knew our destiny, we would certainly know our nature — but if, on the other hand, we knew our nature entirely, we would not necessarily know our destiny. The latter is of another order and belongs to another sphere, which might escape us. Knowledge of the whole trumps knowledge of the parts,

but the opposite does not hold: we may know some determinate parts of a whole while remaining ignorant of others.

11 This, to say nothing of orthodox criticism, is what the Scherers and Renans of the world have clearly shown. "Put the question however you wish," Scherer wrote,

> the result will always be that Christianity differs from Hellenism in that it is a religion; it is a religion because it presumes a supernatural origin, and because its virtue derives precisely from this revealed character.... Hellenism is something great and beautiful, but it is only philosophy; it is condemned to remain without influence on the masses, indeed without so much as contact with them — an object of admiration and spiritual nourishment for a vanishing elite of mankind. Accordingly, what is irrational represents a force, whereas what is purely human and reasonable is sterile.

It can't be said better than that. And so, if we wished, we would demonstrate — and as fully as possible — the "beauties" of Hellenistic culture in general, and of Stoicism in particular. It might be established that Christian dogmas are nothing but a Greek graft on a Judaic trunk. But that's already enough to change the nature of the sap. The task, then, is to determine not just how — in what measure, and for what reason — Christianity adopted ideas from Greek philosophy, but in virtue of what inner principle it organized and recast them for its own use and in its own image.

It's the same as the fact that we do not *become* the meat and plants from which we draw sustenance: we assimilate them and, "by virtue of the guiding idea" that preserves our type within us, we convert them into blood and *humanity*.

12 *Discours sur l'Histoire universelle*, Part. II, ch. 28.

13 These observations, which I did not consider particularly bold, scandalized the learned exegetes of *Revue chrétienne, Temps, and Journal de Genève*. Perhaps they are the same! "But how!" they exclaimed,

> exegesis, the glory of the nineteenth century, the queen of the philological sciences — Lessing, Paulus, de Wette, Strauss, Baur, Schwegler, Ewald, Olshausen, Lepsius, Rawlinson, Burnouf, and Renan himself — all the Egyptologists, Assyriologists, Indologists, Hebraists, philologists,

lexicographers, ethnographers, and anthropologists who have renewed the face of history and, in a certain sense, the very idea we have of the human spirit — that's the treatment they get!

They could have added more. They still may, if they wish:

And the one who treats them this way is one of their disciples, indeed, one of their pupils — one of those ungrateful children, as La Bruyère said, "who beat their nurse!" This is a man who has accomplished the little he has done only in their wake, following their footsteps, by borrowing their principles and methods!

And I agree with them. Moreover, I grant that, after works of general natural history, there are none I have read — none that I still read — as gladly, or with greater reward, than books of exegesis. Need I repeat it, if I've said it some twenty times? One of the most wonderful works of the century, from which I have learned the most, is Eugène Burnouf's *Introduction to the History of Indian Buddhism;* and, of all of Renan's writings, there is none I prefer to his *History of the Semitic Languages.* What a shame it remained unfinished!

And yet, I persist in my declaration. Truth be told, I am not explaining it so much as putting a finer point on it.

There is only one question to be settled — and when I say that there is only one, I mean there are not two. *Is Jesus Christ God or not?* One circles around the question, equivocating and repeating the words of J.-J. Rousseau: "If the life and death of Socrates are those of a sage, the life and death of Jesus are those of a God" — nothing more than a phrase! Yet there is no way to escape the fact that an answer is necessary — either a "yes" or a "no" — and I maintain that, far from aiding us, exegesis only serves the purpose of evasion. Once formulated clearly, this question entails all others— without excepting even revelation or the supernatural — as should surely be plain; yet so long as one has not posed it, nothing has been accomplished at all.

Indeed, let us grant that the conclusions drawn by rationalist exegesis are true, and let us consider them settled once and for all. Let us concede that, since the third or the fourth century, Christianity has been propagated, developed, and supported by human means alone. Let us suppose that Christian dogma, metaphysics, and morality are nothing but "adaptations" of Greek philosophy to the demands of the biblical text. Let us agree that the Gospels were neither written by the authors nor belong to the times to which Church tradition assigns them. What is the result? Is it any less true that, at some point, on the shores of the Lake of Gennesaret, there appeared a man who thought and declared himself the son of God, and that he was believed? Does this change the general character of his teaching or what he preached at the core, does it alter its essential tenor? Is what he did diminished in any way? If not, the question remains in its entirety. As has been said, it is simple: "Was he or was he not God?"

This is what Bossuet meant. It is impossible make the question of Jesus' divinity depend on squabbles about grammar or chronology, and the credibility of the Gospels has nothing to do with the problem of the "supernatural." If Jesus was not God, then we have the right to deny his "mission" and his "miracles." But if he was, his divinity makes his "miracles" and "mission" probable. In either case, exegesis — whether orthodox or rationalist — must already have taken a side one way or the other, even before pursuing its investigations. Or, to put it still another way: exegesis can find, in the conclusions it reaches, only what was already there in the premises it adopted — and the main one is, alternately, the affirmation or negation of the Christ's divinity.

14 *Nouvelle Vie de Jésus*, préface de l'auteur, p. IX.

15 This is the only expression I would agree to modify, since its brevity makes it too absolute. If odious consequences have been drawn from "unsophisticated Darwinism," others may be drawn from more sophisticated Darwinism. I will endeavor to show as much shortly.

16 How deep and how far does this "movement" reach? Here, too, illusions have been attributed to me that, as I have stated quite clearly, I do not entertain. As for the "movement's" existence, it can be denied only by those who are afraid of "popularizing" it in some way by combating it too openly. "Neo-Catholicism" is a fact, to use the language of scientists. A fact can hold more or less importance — but what scientists should already know is that one must always account for it.

17 It was long, long ago that Saint Vincent of Lerins developed the perspective offered here, in his *Commonitorium*. Bossuet presented it again in the first two and in the sixth of his *Avertissements aux Protestants*. Closer to our own day, the man who would become Cardinal Newman made it the subject of a whole book, *Essay on the Development of Christian Doctrine* (1845). In this work, he makes the very subtle — but wholly valid — distinction

between an idea's development and its "perversion" or "corruption." What is more, the features, or signs, he deems characteristic for the distinction warrant notice, for they are all analogies drawn from natural history. In fact, given when he wrote this work, I dare affirm that, in this respect, he paved the way — or even anticipated — the "evolution" of Herbert Spencer and Darwin. Indeed, an element of the same was already present in the work of Saint Vincent of Lerins.

Finally, anyone wishing to know Catholic and Protestant perspectives on this infinitely delicate and weighty matter — which concerns the future of Christian dogma, after all — may consult, on the former, the treatise by Cardinal Franzelin, *De divina traditione et scriptura* (Rome, 1882, third edition, pp. 278-288), and, on the latter, M. Sabatier's interesting brochure, *L'Évolution des Dogmes* (Paris, 1889).

18 On the "socialist" movement, which Leo XIII, after due reflection, seems to have made his own in the celebrated encyclical, *De conditione opificum* — in order to contain, develop, and guide it in a manner conforming to Catholic tradition — the best book I know is M. Nitti's *Le Socialisme catholique*, which Guillaumin has recently published in French translation as part of the series *Collection d'auteurs étrangers contemporains.*

19 A journalist, who is also a Hebraist of some sort, thought to put me in an awkward position by asking where Renan could possibly have expressed such a preposterous idea. He does so in his *Histoire du peuple d'Israël*, t. I, pp. 79-80.

> It must not be forgotten that the chapter Beresith was science for the day in which it was written. The old Babylonian spirit breathes in it still. The succession of creations and ages of the world, the idea that the world has a *becoming*, a history, in which each state proceeds from the previous state by organic development, was an immense advance…. The factitious simplicity of the biblical narrative *has masked the powerful evolutionary spirit that lies at its base, but the genius of the unknown Darwins Babylon possessed 4,000 years ago is still evident*….

And elsewhere (*Israël*, t. II, pp. 387-388) he writes:

> This beautiful page [the narrative of creation] is a first attempt to explain the beginning of the world, *implying a very correct notion of the successive developments of the universe.* Everything invites us to seek the origin of this cosmogonic theory in Babylon. What characterized Babylonian science was the effort to ex-

plain the universe by physical principles. *Spontaneous generation and the progressive transformation of beings were always the order of the day there.*

As for the text by Haeckel, whose existence the same journalist doubted, I refer the reader to the first edition of the French translation (1874), *Histoire de la création naturelle*, pp. 35 et 36.

20 That "exegesis has nothing to offer when faced with revelation," and why this is the case, I endeavored to show in an earlier note; see pp. 71-73. The same arguments, or arguments of the same kind, would demonstrate that "physics can offer nothing to explain the miraculous." After all, the absolute necessity of laws of nature is merely a *postulate* that we require in order to lay the foundations of science, and there is nothing to prove that this *postulate* amounts to anything more than the expression of an entirely relative law governing our intelligence. By the same token, the notion of the "contingency of nature's laws" has been making its way even into metaphysics for a few years now; it should be obvious that it is an abuse of reason to deny the supernatural on the basis of experience as new and short-lived as our own.

21 I appreciate how this statement naturally affected some believers. "The divinity of Jesus Christ is not a matter of demonstration," Mgr d'Hulst has

responded in an article in the *Revue du clergé français*, "one affirms or denies it; either one believes or one does not." But why does one ultimately believe? The least student of theology will tell you that faith, without a doubt, is the freely given assent of the spirit under the impulsion of divine grace. Yet this assent is granted to the word of God, and before the believer can give anything to himself, he must be sure that God has truly spoken. That the divine teaching itself is accessible to reason, like immortality of the soul, or inaccessible, like the mystery of the Trinity, makes no difference. From the moment that God has taught it, I must believe — yet the question whether God has offered instruction is a matter of fact, and what I do to resolve it belongs to the order of rationality. *This is demonstrating the divinity of Jesus Christ ...*

> We must marvel, first, at such ignorance of the nature of faith in a man who has spent so much time with Bossuet. M. Brunetière holds a second surprise in store by classifying the immortality of the soul and the existence of God among matters not subject to demonstration. If anything else is lacking, it is philosophy.

I won't dwell on the disagreeable nature of these last words; truth be told, Mgr d'Hulst is being quite condescending. I wasn't expecting a lesson like this from him; indeed, I find it rather pedantic. That said, it's enough for me to point out to Mgr d'Hulst that if I had understood nature and the relations between "reason" and "faith" as he does — that is, as is done in Catholicism — I would not have written, on the same page, "we will not sacrifice... our independence of thought." What need would there be for me to "reserve" the independence of my thought if I accepted the teaching of the Church in its integrality? It would have sufficed to declare myself "Catholic," pure and simple. Nor would I have written "[i]t is not science's place to undermine or strengthen 'proofs of religion.'"

And so, however lacking my philosophical instruction may be, I continue to hold that "neither the immortality of the soul nor the existence of God is to be demonstrated." That was Pascal's view, and it was also Kant's — and I have every right to be "wrong" in their company! The rights of what used to be called "the errant conscience" must be preserved. I do not consider God's existence to be a matter either of proofs drawn from the order of the world or of the proofs one may derive from the idea of the perfect or the infinite — "whose essence implies existence, *cujus essentia involvit existentiam*"; nor, finally, does it involve proofs drawn from the presence of the moral law within us. Indeed, after having lent the matter much more thought than Mgr d'Hulst thinks, I can only see "tautologies" here. Those who find these proofs "demonstrative" fail to note that they all imply a God "perceptible to the heart" and affirmed by Him before being, I wouldn't say "demonstrated" by reasoning, so much as even conceived by reason. Or, to put it differently, one already knows God when one attempts to prove His existence, and I consider, for myself — that is, based on personal experience, which is the sole authority I am able to invoke — that no proof can create it in hearts that do not feel it.

I say the same of "immortality of the soul" — it cannot be established by any argument that does not, itself, apply to all living beings in addition to man, or, conversely, by an argument that allows for the greater part of human beings to be excluded. On this matter, one may consult any number of theorists in Switzerland, Germany, England, and America — who are little known in France — of what is called "conditional immortality."

As for the "nature of faith," there can be no doubt I would not presume to discuss the definition given by the Church; what is more, and unlike M. Taine, I am far from considering it to be what Mgr d'Hulst calls "holy enthusiasm or delirium." However, I acknowledge that in recognizing in faith an adherence to truths conceived as "rational," I do see it as an act or decision of the will before all else. Nowhere have I claimed that one "believes without reason to believe"; still, it does not seem to me that such "reason" or "reasons" are intellectual in nature. One believes because one wants to believe — for reasons of a moral order: one senses the need for a rule and discerns that neither nature nor man can offer one independently. For all that, what is difficult — or impossible — is to make oneself feel this need; in this sense, one does not give oneself faith.

22 One day, perhaps, I will attempt to say how I conceive of the reciprocal relations between morality and religion as they have varied over history. For the moment, however, I believe I have stated clearly enough that religion and morality have not always constituted a unity. There can be no doubt, for instance, that Greek morality resulted from the slow and arduous conquest of polytheism by philosophy; and if Ernest Renan's *History of the People of Israel* warrants belief, one could — and one should — say as much of Judaic morality. All the same, Scherer remains in the right against freethinkers of M. Berthelot's stripe. "The conscience is like the heart, and it needs a beyond!" Or, still more — and just as matter in an alloy or a

given combination in nature possesses and develops properties that are not contained in its elements — the alliance between morality and religion gives each one social value and import that neither one could have in isolation.

23 *Études sur la littérature contemporaine,* t. VIII, p. 182, 183.

24 Quoted in W. H. Mallock, *Is Life Worth Living?* p. 81, 82.

25 If one credited certain philosophers and scholars — for example, M. Charles Richet's article in the *Revue Rose,* written in response to the work at hand — one would have to say the opposite. In consequence, the morality of solidarity, for instance, would "pose" itself only by "opposing" the morality of Christianity by a *process* of continuous differentation and advancement. I cannot refrain from transcribing here an eloquent passage from M. Richet's article. "What ideas about morality," he exclaims,

> did Bossuet have about war, slavery, torture, freedom of conscience, the equality of mankind, and respect for human life? And what ideas do we have today? What judgment did Bossuet pronounce on the *dragonnades*, St. Bartholomew's Day and

the Inquisition — and what judgments are made today?

The answer to these questions, which are a little too self-assured, is easy enough. In the *Abrégé de l'histoire de France*, written for the Dauphin — and in part by the latter himself, whose "history essay" Bossuet was sometimes content merely to correct — one may read what is said of St. Bartholomew's:

> To impress the conspiracy on the popular mind all the more, acts of thanksgiving were made to God for the supposed discovery. *These displays did not impress anyone, and all respectable people detested the action performed all the more* because it was impossible to conceive a pretext slighter in plausibility. *Its horror mounted with each day as news arrived from the provinces.*

And, a little further on, about the death of Charles IX:

> He died in a strange manner: horrifying convulsions seized him, and his pores opened wide through movements so violent that blood poured out everywhere. One did not fail to note that *it was justice for a prince who had so cruelly spilled his subjects' blood to bathe in his own.*

Isn't it better to have read Bossuet before speaking of him?

Then, there would be no need to wonder what his "ideas about war" were. One would be familiar with *Politics Drawn from Holy Scripture*, where, in the chapter entitled "God Does Not Love War," the following words stand:

> God refused David His acceptance [to build the Temple] out of hatred for the blood in which He saw his hands already steeped. So much saintliness in this prince was not able to efface the stain. God loves the peaceable, and the glory of peace He prefers over that of arms, however holy and religious.

On the other hand, it is the scholars and scientists who have proclaimed the "holiness of war" with their false interpretation of the struggle for life. Still more, if anyone has made it the school of all virtues in our own day, it was a learned party of another kind: Field Marshal von Moltke. M. Charles Richet does not personally embody all "Science" as a whole, and I know a number of learned individuals who do not fill the ranks of the *Ligue de la paix*.

Need I now justify Bossuet apropos of "respect for human life" or "slavery"? It will be enough for me to remark that the justification — or excuse — he provides for slavery is founded, precisely, on what is deemed the sacred quality of human life, *servus a servando*: for Bossuet, the slave is the vanquished, whose life the vanquisher has respected. Conversely, it would pose no difficulty to quote learned parties — illustrious scholars such as Agassiz — who, in our own day, have based slavery on the "inequality of human races," that is, on reasons which belong to the order of anatomy and physiology and, in consequence, count as "scientific."

Yet M. Richet also says: "The morality the Church teaches today is likely not very different from the morality science teaches." The very opposite has just been shown. To begin with, the morality of the Church differs from that of the sciences inasmuch as its fundamental doctrine of solidarity between all human beings has nothing scientific about it at all — it has nothing in common with the doctrine of the "struggle for existence." More still, the Church's teaching differs from science's for having preceded it by some fifteen- or seventeen hundred years; therefore, when "Science" did not yet exist, it provided for the moral needs of mankind. But most of all, the difference lies in its having located the moral ideal in the perfection of the individual — for which M. Charles Richet, along with many others, can only find a place in the progress of the species. This is what has prompted him to formulate a strange definition: "Evil... is the pain of others"! One might as well say that we have duties only towards those like us — and that if they do not suffer from our manner of acting, we enjoy every license to satisfy our worst instincts: *indulgere turpissimae corporis parti*. Thus did an ancient author qualify our nether region.

Evidently, M. Charles Richet, who didn't bother to read Bossuet before waving him against me, also failed, in his haste to offer a riposte, to gauge the import of what he said. This is further proof that questions of this kind cannot be answered at the drop of a hat. In short order, I will provide still other examples.

26 In spite of these words, a few Protestants were moved by what follows a bit more than is reasonable, and, in their *Revues and Journaux* — particularly in Paris and Geneva — they have responded with the rigid disdain that characterizes them all too often. I'm almost afraid I will appear to lack dignity by calling to mind how I have always spoken of them.

The truth is, I've never granted that one owes them "tolerance." On the contrary, I've always maintained that Calvin might well have ceded it to Torquemada alone — and in terms of "intolerance," at that. If anything, consult his *Refutation of the Errors of Michael Servetus*. Moreover, on the matter of the Protestants' changes of opinion — which they now seem to want to excuse as a regrettable lack of logic and consistency, and now to boast of, as dazzling proof of their complete freedom of thought — I take Bossuet's side. This is also the side of historical truth, as one can see in M. Rébelliau's admirable book, *Bossuet historien du protestantisme*. Still, I think I have praised them enough. "Intolerant and proud," I wrote less than three years ago,

> intractable, dejected, and morose, contemptuous and austere, affecting piety down to the very clothes they wore, Protestants ... possessed the virtue for which these faults were the covering, as it were; yet thanks to it one may affirm that in 1685, and for more than a century, *they represented the moral fiber of France*.... Removed from temptation by the same measures that removed them from the trades, they erected, in the society of the age of Louis XIV, a living doctrine, so to speak, by the ardor of their faith, their constant concern for salvation, their distance from ready pleasures,

the dignity of their mores, indeed, by the very
inflexibility and the pride of their bearing.

Instead of committing the abuse of quoting myself,
I refer the reader to the study, *Sur la formation de
l'idée de progrès*, from which these lines are drawn.
And yet, our Protestants are never content — as if
the very name they bear imposed the obligation always to "protest"; and, although their purview is
assuredly much superior in France to the power of
Catholics in Germany or England, for example, as
soon as one speaks of them freely, it seems they are
offended. Whatever "liberalism" they boast of, one
never sees them free from a confessional point of
view. What they have the greatest difficulty understanding, is that anyone — as I have attempted to
do in the two or three pages that follow — should
consider "Protestantism" and "Catholicism" histor-
ically and attempt to discuss them with as much independence, disregard for dogma, and liberty as one
might speak of "Alexandrism" or "Stoicism."

27 Macaulay, *Essais philosophiques*, trad. G. Guizot,
p. 275.

28 It has been objected that there can be no "government" in matters of conscience, yet the question
remains. To demonstrate its significance in a few
words: if conscience forbade me from bearing

arms or paying taxes, I would like to know what "government," today, would respect my scruples. Moreover, it suffices that the governance of men's consciences occur without coercion to be perfectly legitimate.

29 Did I perhaps fail to explain myself clearly? At any rate, the phrase — "... and when hope founders, in turn charity sinks" — has been taken to mean that *charitable institutions* can supposedly exist in the bosom of Catholicism alone. Is one to *capitalize* or *italicize* everything? Take a sentence like the following: "*Faith* destroys *Hope* in his heart; and when *Hope* founders, in turn *Charity* sinks." How is it possible not to have seen that something altogether different was at issue? It astonishes me even now. At any rate, what I meant to say, I will now repeat more fully:

1. *On the article of Protestantism:* although it stands beyond doubt that the principal concern for Protestants, as for Catholics, is salvation, the Protestant necessarily lacks reasons for the trust the Catholic places, first, in the "infinite indulgence of his God," second, in the "sacramental virtue of confession," and third, in the "merit of works" — his own and even those of others. The God of Luther and Calvin is a jealous God, inspiring more fear than love. On the other hand, the disquiet, remorse, and terror for

which the Catholic finds comfort in confession, automatically grow, as it were, in the Protestant's soul. Inasmuch as the soul of the Protestant bears full responsibility for itself, it carries all the weight of the sin that besets it. Finally, since "works" are useless — in this context, I mean "practices" — it finds assistance only inasmuch as it prevails against itself. I do not deny that there results a superior moral bearing, if I may put it this way; indeed, I remember that fourteen or fifteen years ago, I scandalized a few Catholics when I wrote, in a study on the great English novelist George Eliot, "that French naturalism would always lack the moral value that *three centuries of vigorous Protestant education* have infused, as it were, into English naturalism." My view has not changed on this point of literary history or on the more general question at issue here. Still, it should now be clear what I mean, "how can one show concern for others when one is worried about oneself to this degree!" Surely, more intense preoccupation with oneself underlies Protestantism than Catholicism; and if Protestants rightly commend themselves for viewing their religion only from a moral angle, what I meant to say — and said — is that the matter looks different when considered from a social angle. That is a vantage point, too!

2. *On the article of Catholicism:* concerning the merit of "works," "indulgences," as well as the solidarity uniting generations among Catholics, I cannot, to please the Protestants, cross out Purgatory from the Church's beliefs; nor can I join in their derision, for I find the idea admirable. On this point, one may reread the *Divine Comedy.* That said, can it be that our own great writers have been forgotten? Is it possible never to have read the *St. Petersburg Dialogues*? Ought I to call to mind the admirable words Joseph de Maistre wrote about *indulgences*? "There is no Protestant father of a family who has not granted indulgences in his own home, who was not pardoned a punishable child, *through the intercession, or through the merits of another child"* — this is Maistre's own emphasis — "with whom he is content."

> There is not a Protestant ruler who has not signed fifty *indulgences* during his reign, in providing a position, or in remitting or committing a punishment, etc., *through the merits* of father, brothers, sons, parents, or ancestors. This principle is so general and so natural that it is always being displayed in the least decrees of human justice. You have laughed a thousand times at the foolish scales that Homer placed in the hands of his Jupiter, apparently to make

him ridiculous. Christianity shows us
quite another set of scales. On one side
are all the crimes, on the other all the
satisfactions; on one side the good works
of all mankind, the sacrifices and the tears
of the innocent accumulating endlessly to
be weighed against the evil that since the
beginning of things has poured its poison-
ous waters into the other basin....

What is immoral here? To take upon oneself the
burden, so to speak, of a beloved being's crime or
vice, its weakness or carelessness? And if one pro-
tests, what is one protesting, if not against what I
would call the doctrine of solidarity in salvation? In
such a case, I was correct to say that the principle of
Catholicism has greater "social fecundity" than that
of Protestantism. I would add that any effort Protestants make to deny as much will only ensconce
them more fully in individualistic affirmations.

Once more, it's plain to see that all of this has nothing to do with finding out whether "charitable institutions" are more numerous and better administrat-
ed in Catholic lands or in Protestant ones.

30 See Taine, *Littérature anglaise*, t. II; *la Renaissance chrétienne*.

31 I will soon explain myself, in *La Moralité de la Doctrine Évolutive*.

32 Th. Ziegler, *Die soziale Frage eine sittliche Frage,* 1890.

33 This question — "should one hope for anything of the kind?" — startled a few people; the reaction offers abundant proof of the confusion, or anarchy, of ideas among which one debates as best one can. Whether conflict or cooperation, civilization is, at any rate, a "meeting" of forces, and its complexity, which provides the measure of its value, depends on the diversity of forces, above all. This is why I fail to understand anything about the declamation with which Dr. Clémenceau responded to me in *La Justice*. "Your God," he vociferated,

> and your religion are nothing but hypocritical contrivances, miserable means of social defense against the mounting tide of those they used to contain, and who now claim their share of earthly pleasures. The law of Darwin, you dare say, would provide only abominable lessons of conduct. But take a look around. Who is preaching the *laissez-faire* of the struggle for life, if not your Academy economists, your officiants of celestial joys?

In turn, the good socialist responds that there's another natural and scientific law: the law of justice, which the social body — comprised of the power of all — has the duty to impose on the stronger. That's social science at work, milords: the science of justice and liberty, which will topple the dogma of servitude in body and soul. And if you're so eager, after so many vain prophecies, to predict the rout of an enemy who is only multiplying and mounting, it's because you sense that, in the lull of the present, a mighty assault is being readied to cast down the last bastions of the iniquitous order you declare to be divine.

This, if I'm not mistaken, is twofold claptrap, and if it weren't for the menace of the final lines, there would be nothing solid to hold onto in this mass of metaphors as hollow as they are pretentious.

All the same, I will try to do so. I would point out to Dr. Clémenceau that I never uttered a single word in all that I said, to "officiate celestial joys" or, for that matter, to defend "Academy economists," who are also not my responsibility. Nor do I care — and the impartial reader now has the proof before his eyes — whom what I have said may please or displease. My sole concern is to say how I consider, or view, matters — which is surely the first condition of "scientific" research. I venture to add that if there is anyone who has never preached "the *laissez-faire* of the struggle for life," it is I. And Dr. Clémenceau would know as much, if twenty years of preoccupation with political affairs had not made him a stranger, as it were, to the course of ideas in his own times. While Dr. Clémenceau was making and unmaking ministers, I endeavored to study the questions I wanted to treat one day — to discuss which, it may be, neither his political career nor his medical studies have adequately prepared him.

But more remarkable still is the self-certainty with which our doctor arrogates, to his allies and himself, a monopoly on "justice" and "liberty." If, perhaps, we fear this "social science at work" less than he does — indeed, if we cannot conceive a nobler pursuit than to separate it from the obscure origins in which it still seems to be mired, is the least of his concerns. And because he would see in me a defender of "servitude in body and soul," he says so without further "ceremony" and, naturally, tries to make his readers believe it:

> Their every deed, you may believe, is
> nothing but hypocrisy.

That is what he asserts in a doctorial tone (no pun intended) and without the hint of proof (which he does not even try to provide), just because it seems to him — so tolerant is he! — that it's impossible to have ideas other than his own without rousing the suspicion of deficient straightforwardness. I did not "predict" anyone's rout; nor did I write a single word that could lead anyone to believe that I find anything "divine" in the "iniquitous order" he attacks. But what does it matter? He needs to presume as much in order to write his article, whose whole force is constituted by the weakness of arguments he attributes to those at whom he unleashes his eloquence. So he presumes, and off he goes! Such methods are too convenient.

Well, no! If a "social question" exists, it won't be solved by treating it in this manner — nor will it even be posed properly. One should take a closer look. If civilization, as we have said, is nothing but a "meeting" of forces that ought to "fit together" in order to achieve equilibrium, now we will say that one must not fail to acknowledge any of them, or seek to expel them from the "system" in which they, like all others, constitute necessary parts. Is religion one of these forces? That, right there, is the whole problem at issue. But to start out by denying as much in order to resolve the question — that, one must admit, is a strange method. Perhaps, if Dr. Clémenceau has done nothing else in his article, it will turn out that we have already responded to him, and well in advance.

34 After replying, to the best of my ability, to some of the objections this article occasioned, I thought it might be interesting to reproduce here — without betraying the signatories — three or four of the letters it earned me. The first comes from a Catholic, the second from a Protestant, and the third from a freethinker. I should point out that none of the authors is personally known to me.

I.

Monsieur,

... After this article, there will be those in the parliaments who deem you a clericalist, and others, in the sacristies, will expect you at confession; yet there will also be members of the clergy... grateful to you, not out of narrow-minded, partisan interest, but for generous reasons, for having brought spiritual peace....

... We, believers in the Christ, who believe that His morality is divine and, in consequence, adequate to absolute morality; we who, believing in the Church, the extension and organ of the Christ, believe that its charge is to adapt, over the ages, immutable morality to the new needs of mankind and new conditions of life — how could we not have heartfelt, fraternal sentiments toward sincere parties who, without sharing our faith, judge for other reasons that at least in relative terms — relative to the point of development we have attained — the world cannot do without Catholic morality....

II.

Monsieur,

I read with the greatest interest your article in the last issue of *Revue des Deux-Mondes*. It will not surprise you that I do not share all the ideas presented when I tell you I am Protestant, and Protestant by conviction. But before being a Protestant, I am a Christian, or at least I try to be, and as a Christian I am happy to hear a voice... defending the rights of religious truth. Catholic, Protestant — the words no longer suit the times or hold any interest. Ah! If only all those who follow

Jesus Christ could forget them and walk
together to attain eternal truths which have
already transformed the world — and should
transform it more completely still!...

III.

Monsieur,

You have launched an appeal to men of good-
will: permit one of them to tell you why he
will offer his assistance to those who, by all
legitimate means [this is my correspondent's
emphasis] seek to combat the philosophical
concordat that you, a new Bonaparte, went
and signed in Rome in the name of French
thought (provided it may be said to exist in
the *Journal des Débats* and the *Revue des
Deux-Mondes*)...

I'll stop the quotation here; the rest is easy enough
to guess. Yet I cannot resist the pleasure of drawing
attention to a rather curious detail. My correspondent
wrote, in flowing script and with ready hand, "… will
offer his assistance to those who, by all means, seek to
combat the new concordat"; fortunately, however, he
reread his words and added "legitimate" on top: "…
his assistance to those who, by all legitimate means,
seek to combat the new concordat."

THE TRANSLATOR

Erik Butler has translated numerous works from modern European languages, including Léon Bloy's *Disagreeable Tales* and Oskar Panizza's *The Pig in Poetic, Mythological, and Moral-Historical Perspective*. He is also the author of *The Bellum Grammaticale and the Rise of European Literature*, *Metamorphoses of the Vampire in Literature and Film* and *The Rise of the Vampire*.

www.ingramcontent.com/pod-product-compliance
Lightning Source LLC
Chambersburg PA
CBHW071234090426
42736CB00014B/3073